REACH

It's All You Have To Do In Life

Kaz Nascimento

DEDICATED TO

TANYA, KAYLIE, KRISTIN

CONTENTS

INTRODUCTION

For many years I have always thought about being someone great that made a difference in the world. I always wanted to inspire, encourage, and help people win at the game of life but never knew how to, as I was struggling in my own life. I tried through music, radio, and public speaking. Still, I never had the same effects as a Jam Master Jay, a Casey Kassem, or Dr. Martin Luther King. I told myself that they all had to start somewhere, I am sure they dealt with disappointment, embarrassment, and loss, but they never gave up. They stayed strong and had the passion and love to help make a difference. There had to be a point in their lives where those men started to see the first steps of change.

Personally, after my disappointments, embarrassments, and losses, I have finally made it to my first step where change is happening. I have built up the courage and strength to share my story with the world about reaching for my goals and dreams while overcoming many personal obstacles in my life. I know you are asking yourself, what is so special about your story? The answer is that it is not special, and I am not anyone special, and I am just like you. I am not a GOD, I am not better than you, I just happened to choose a different path in life than most, and look at life, the world, and myself from another perspective. I decided to share my story with you to inspire, encourage, and reach. I want to let you know that whatever it is in life you can achieve, you can have, you can do it, and I am living proof of that. As I take you through my journey in this book, you will see that GOD put me in certain situations that I never understood until now. The pain I encountered, the heartaches, the blood, the sweat, and the tears, were all part of GOD'S plan. GOD used me and continues to use me as a vehicle to help others who are currently dealing with the same situations. Understand that you are not alone. Know that there is someone else out there that understands you and is cheering you on to reach the finish line of life.

This book is not only about my story, but your story as well, and you may see yourself in my situations that may be relatable. Every one of us has a story to tell if you think it is necessary or not, and the truth is your story is needed. I want to take a moment to thank those that genuinely believe in what I stand for in life, those that have supported me and continue to help me in my career, and those that have loved me and those that have seen the good in all I do.

I am not writing this book to make money, I am not writing this book to be famous, and I am not writing this book to make a point or prove a point. I am writing this book to inspire, encourage, and hope to help you see your dreams and goals come to life. I am writing this book from deep within my heart and soul and being as truthful to you about my story. Some may agree, some may disagree, and some may not understand my story at all. I know that we cannot please everyone in this world, but what we can do in this world is anything we want. We can be the Jam Master Jay's, and we can be the Casey Kassem's and the MLK's. We must believe and reach.

REACH

I HAD A VISION

In life, we all have visions, something we can picture. Maybe you are in that new car, what about that new home you always drive by on your block, that beautiful girl or guy you want to be with that would fulfill your love. Those are considered visions, and as humans, we picture things in life that we truly wish to have but only think about. The question is, how can we make them a reality? Are you ready for the answer? "REACH." That is all you must do in life, it is just "REACH" for the things you want, and it is that simple.

In 2003 when my father passed away, I cleaned out his apartment and came across a letter I wrote to him when I was about eight years old. What I was about to read was going to blow my mind and maybe at this moment yours as well. The letter stated that one day I would be a "ROCK STAR." I was going to take care of him, live in a big home, and have lots of money. I had a vision at eight years old, and I brought it to life.

Ok I am not an actual "ROCK STAR" I do not live in a multimillion-dollar home or have my bank account oozing out with tons of money. Still, I have accomplished what I visioned over 30 years. I was a recognized local radio host and night club DJ. I have had my share of the money, vehicles, owned a condo, and lived in 2 homes simultaneously. I guess you can say to an extent I'm a "ROCK STAR in my own right.

We all are "ROCKSTARS, we all can achieve greatness in life, we can all make our dreams come true, all you have to do is just "REACH" I'm living proof that it can happen. Never let anyone tell you that you cannot because you can. Yes, certain circumstances keep us from moving forward to our visions and goals but remember this, that place and time play a big part as you head down your road of destiny. GOD will let you know when the time is right, and GOD will never lead you down the wrong path. You may question the path your put on, but never question where you are going to end up because it will lead you to what you have envisioned in your own life.

When I was in the 5th grade, I will never forget an incident that forever changed my life. As an adult, I now understand that it was part of GOD'S plan and the road that I needed to travel to get to where I am today. I had a teacher named Mrs. Anthony, a powerful and firm black woman that did not take any mess. She towered over the class, standing about 5' 10" with salt and peppered hair, slim built, and most people feared her. I once forgot to turn in my math homework, and Mrs. Anthony was not at all pleased. She made me get up in front of the class as she proceeded to embarrass me and shouted, "Class, you see this person here? This person is going to flip your burgers and pump your gas" My peers let out a huge laugh, and I ran back to my desk, trying to hold back the embarrassment and tears. After that day, I no longer cared about school, my education, or my life. Still, as you can see, GOD had bigger and better plans for me, not an easy path but a path to success with a vision and a purpose.

MY FAMILY

I was born in Oakland, California, and moved around quite a bit throughout the bay area, never staying in one place for more than a couple of years. I grew up in a household where we rarely mentioned the word "LOVE." If it was said, it was said without meaning, it was just another word that never registered with anyone. Still, to this day, I have a hard time telling any of my family members that I love them, and they have a hard time telling me as well. You know the saying, "Home is where the heart is," the heart was never in my house as it was destroyed with lies, drugs, and alcohol.

My parents divorced when I was about five years old. My Father, a Vietnam Veteran who was dealing with his own demons after the war, and my Mother, who was from the Philippine Islands, had difficulty adjusting to life in America. My parents met in the Philippines when my Dad was stationed there during the Vietnam War in the late '60s. I am not sure the truth about how they met, but I heard stories from a strip bar to a Marine picnic, and I may never know the truth.

I have two older siblings, my brother Bill and my sister Julie. Julie is my half-sister from a previous relationship my Mom had before she married my Dad. We were not the family next door. I thought all the dysfunction was normal until I grew older and met other families and realized we were not normal. My Dad probably dealt with the most issues that affected us as a family. He turned to drugs and alcohol to deal with his pain from the war and even attempted suicide on several occasions. He fought so many personal demons that he did not know how to deal with them. My Dad was physically and verbally abusive to my Mom and my older brother. I remember many times hiding in the closet with my eyes closed, whenever my Dad would physically abuse my Mom or brother, it terrified me. My Dad never was physically abusive to me, not sure why, but he eventually told me the alarming reason later in life. He told me that he had to kill kids that looked like me in Vietnam. He carried the pain of that for the rest of his life, and it haunted him.

My father and I rekindled our relationship in the last few years of his life. He was a good man but dealt with so much pain that most of us would never really understand. I will always remember the day He passed away. He came from California to visit my family and me in Seattle, Washington, but our visit was short-lived. My Dad had passed away from heart failure in his hotel room, where I found his lifeless body lying on the bed. I must have just sat there for a few minutes at the edge of the bed in silence before calling anyone. Our last words I got to speak to him the night before he passed was "I love you," as he replied with, "I'm proud of you son."

THE BEATING

I think my Mom did the best she could as a single parent raising three kids. She worked a lot, so I never got to see her or spend a lot of time with her growing up, and still, to this day, I rarely see her. I was the baby of the family, and it seemed like my brother and sister took priority over me. My Mom gave them whatever they wanted, cars, money, clothes, and she did whatever they asked, and I did feel a little jealous and left out. My brother and sister spent more time and had more of a relationship with my Mom than I did and never understood why. I once asked my Mom if I went to jail, would she bail me out. Her response was, "You will be fine," not the words I was expecting to hear from my own Mother. I felt our relationship was never really in a great place or if it will ever be. Sometimes I feel like she regretted having me. I was once told she only had me to help her marriage with my Dad.

After my parents divorced, my Mom was struggling as a single parent. She started to date a man named Joe, who became a glorified babysitter to us, which turned out to be a bad decision. He was much older than my Mom, a husky man with salt and peppered hair and a gentleman's mustache. She ended up staying with him for about ten years, and over those years, I was exposed to things that I did not understand as a child and a teenager. Time eventually revealed Joe's real side. He was a drug dealer, child abuser, and manipulated people. I even once watched him sucker-punch my Mom in the face. I remember my encounters with him, and he once told me in a stern voice, "YOU EITHER CALL ME DAD OR MR. COSGROVE" I was not at all cool with that.

I remember I came home from school one day, and he was waiting for me at the door with his belt with a look of frustration. The school had called my home to say I have been doing very poorly. Keep in mind school was never my thing, plus later in life, I found out I had a learning disability and never got help for it until It was too late. Joe had sent me to my room where it was dark, and he proceeded to beat me senseless with his thick leather brown belt. He came in every hour on the hour to whip me, and I was wondering when it was going to stop. I shouted out, "PLEASE STOP," as I endured it for almost 6 hours. I never felt so helpless in my life, and no one in my home tried to stop it. The pain, the welts, the redness all over my body, was unbearable. I did not sleep that night. I would doze off for a bit here and there but would always be alert for when Joe came in for the next beating.

About a week later, my Mom made me move with Joe to a small city called Red Bluff, north of the bay area, four hours away, where I lived with Joe for the next year. I did not think anything of it, but now I realized as an adult that my Mom had abandoned me as a child. I would only see her maybe once a month if that, she would come and visit for a few days then head back to the bay area where my brother and sister were living with her. I was alone with this crazy man and his wild ways. He once even tried to abuse me sexually. I had no one to talk to, no one to trust, or anyone to be there for me.

WHO AM I

As weird or as funny as this may sound, I wanted to be
"WHITE" growing up. As a kid, Caucasian people seem to
have it all, money, homes, beautiful families, and
everything in life going their way. I had a hard time
growing up being a mix of Filipino and Portuguese. It was
not the "in-thing" growing up. I was embarrassed about
who I was and never proud of my cultures as I only heard
the negative things. As Asians, we never had any role
models to look up to like the white folks. All we ever had
was terrible jokes about being bad drivers, only could
afford flip flops, and our food stinks. As far as the
Portuguese side, I knew nothing, and I did not even know
where it was on the map. I started to become influenced by
other people I hung out with and tried to find myself in
their cultures.

I hung around many Black folks and Mexicans growing up and adapted to their culture and lifeways. For once in my life, I thought I might have found a place of acceptance and love by being like these people I hung around. I found out quickly that this was not who I was or what I represented. I had a hard time finding myself, who I was, what I stood for, and who I was supposed to be. I was indeed a lost soul with no guidance and no understanding of life at all. All I knew was what my friends were doing and what I saw on TV and in the movies.

I don't think I truly accepted who I was and my culture until I was almost in my mid 20's. I took it upon myself to understand where I came from and my family history. I was intrigued by what I found, and it made me proud of who I was. I tell you today, be proud of who you are, be proud of your culture, be proud of where you are from. Never be embarrassed or worry about who you are. Love yourself and stand tall with your head up high and accept the person you are because you are one of a kind.

NO SHOES

Fast forward a few years to when I was 16, I left home and moved in with my brother Bill, another bad mistake. This is where I learned to grow up quick. I went from the age of 16 to 21 in a matter of months. I was living back in Oakland, California, in maybe one of the city's worst areas. It was here I learned street life, drugs, sex, and now life with no parental supervision. My brother was using drugs heavily at the time, drinking, and was never home. There was no food, no phone, and no electricity at times.

I went to school in a city called Alameda, a nicer area, about 10 minutes away from Oakland. I had to take the city bus to get there. I would wake up at 4:30 am and catch the bus around 5:30 to get to school by 7 am. It made for a long day, and I had to do the same thing at the end of the day, so you can imagine it was dark when I left and dark when I got home at about 6 pm. It was getting old, and I wanted to finish school, but I did not have the money to get back and forth two times a day, five days a week. That is when I knew I was done with school and was never going to get out of here.

I recall I went to pick up a girl that I was dating at the time from school. Michelle was her name, the first girl I ever fell in love with, and my first serious relationship. She went to a Catholic school in the heart of the city in downtown Oakland right off East 14th Street, which was notorious for everything and anything that could go wrong. Sure enough, that day, it did for me. I was with a buddy of mine, Carl Johnson, a skinny, goofy but good-hearted guy dealing with his life issues like me. He came with me that day to pick up my girlfriend. We had no car, so we walked a good 3 or 4 miles from my house to the school. As we approached the crosswalk, we noticed three exceptionally clean and unique 1964 Chevy Impala lowriders that stopped at the traffic light in front of us as we crossed the street. Carl and I thought the cars were awesome, and as we made our way onto the sidewalk, the traffic light changed for the opposite traffic. We noticed the three low riders pulled up alongside us and got out of the cars. Ignoring the comments made by a skinny Hispanic male, that shouted "COME HERE FOOL" before we realized, 16 Hispanic guys surrounded us.

Not sure what was happening or what we had done, but this did not look good. Carl was ready to fight, and before I knew it, he took a few punches to the face. Not sure who pushed us, but me and Carl were dropped to the hard concrete. As I laid there on the cold hard cement, I noticed one of the guys had a gun. I yelled to Carl, "JUST GIVE THEM YOUR STUFF." It lasted all about 2 minutes, but it seemed like forever. The thugs ran back to their cars, laughing and yelling as they sped off with not a care in the world, weaving back into traffic like nothing happened.

After it was all over, I looked at Carl as he was bleeding from his mouth and I asked if he was ok, he replied I'm fine, and then a snicker came on his face as he let out a little laugh and said, "Where are your shoes?" I looked down, and sure enough, they were gone. I guess during the whole incident, I did not even notice they were gone. We still picked up my girlfriend that day, but I was embarrassed, walking back home with no shoes.

THE CHOICE

When I was 17, I eventually moved away from California. I made my way to Seattle, Washington, where I reconnected with my Mom and lived with her. It was quite a culture shock, and I had to adjust, no more sunshine, it always rained, and it was freezing. I remember my Mom had bought me a plane ticket, and I had never been on a plane before in my life or even been to Seattle. At first, I was scared and unsure of what to expect. I was leaving the only place I knew and all my friends and family. I kept thinking that I am ready to start a new chapter in my life, and I hope this was the chance to better myself.

My mind and body were not in a good state, and I was malnourished. At 5'6", I weighed 99 pounds and felt like a Prisoner of War coming home after many years of being hidden from the world. All I had was a backpack of clothes and a small box of some of my stuff I got to salvage when I lived with my brother. I am not going to lie, I hated living in Seattle. It seemed like life was moving slower, and the people were fake, but you must remember, I just came from a fast-paced life where you had to be on your toes, and I was not thinking like a typical 17-year-old.

I recall my Mom enrolled me in a High School there, and since I was the new kid from California, everyone wanted to know about me. All I ever heard from people was, "I have family in California," "I went there once," blah blah blah. Still, in my mind, these people have no idea what I just endured over the last year of my life. My days finishing High School ended that day as I was approached by two guys that claimed they were gang members. They asked where I was from, and I said, "Not from here," they proceeded to interrogate me like the police asking me tons of questions. One of the guys was leaning up against a payphone. I walked over to it, and he got into position like I was going to fight him. I reached my hand out and picked up the receiver and called my Mom. I said, "Mom, come get me, this place is whack" I hung up the phone and walked away and out of the school like a boss. I may have set a record for the shortest enrollment in a High School that day, one period. As I looked back at the two guys, they just stood there in silence, not understanding what just happened. I would have to admit I was amused the whole time and chuckled a bit at the situation.

I moved back to California a month later, where I stayed for about a year with my Aunt, Uncle and Cousins, then came back to Seattle. After bouncing around from house to house and not having any stability in my life, I was ready to find some, and eventually, I did. Years later, I completed my schooling, got my G.E.D., went to college, enlisted in the Military, and even spent time in Law Enforcement. It was not an easy run, but eventually, I did it and am proud of not giving up. There were times I wanted to give up and give in, there were times I could not find the strength to continue, but I did. I am sure you are asking yourself what it was that drove me and pushed me to continue when most people in these situations would have given up. I looked back on my life and said to myself, I never want to live that way again. I did not want to have a family and show them what I was exposed to, I did not want to be without, and most of all, I did not want negative things to outweigh the good things in life. I liked having peace, that stability, and, most of all, that love in life that I so longed for.

WHY

I know understanding life can be a difficult thing to comprehend. Why are we here? What is my mission? Why is this happening to me? What is it that I am supposed to be doing? Those are questions only we as individuals can answer. Still, whatever it is, there is an answer and a purpose, and just like the song by Bob Dylan, the answer is blowing in the wind.

If you follow your heart, you will find your purpose, your passion, and yourself in the process. For me, it was hard to piece all these things together, but just like a puzzle, over time, it all came together like a beautiful picture that made sense. Start with yourself, love who you are, be proud of who you are, be proud of your culture, family, where you are from, and never be ashamed of who you are. Do not stop believing in yourself, do not stop believing in others because they have a story too and a purpose which may not be the same as yours, but for someone else like them in this world.

MY HEALTH

After many years of pain, hurt, blood, sweat, and tears, life eventually caught up to me. I recall it was December of 2010, about a few weeks from Christmas, one of the most stressful times of the year for many. I was currently working on my film documentary that was all going to hell. I was having issues with my boss at work at the radio station that did not like me, and I was financially in a bind trying to take care of my family. It was on my way home that night after my shift at the station, and all that evening, I felt like I was in a weird fog or funk that I could not shake.

As I started driving home, I felt this bizarre sensation hit my body like I just drank 30 cups of coffee. My head felt light, and my heart was beating like I just ran a marathon. I honestly thought I was having a heart attack. I went numb, and I screamed as my entire body went into shock. I called my wife Tanya at home and woke her up, telling her that something was not right. She told me to calm down and go to the hospital if I needed to. I did drive to the hospital but circled in the parking lot, still very confused about what was happening to me. I ended up going home and decided to sleep it off. I made it home safe and sound, laid in bed and took a sleep aid to calm me down and hope it would all be over in the morning. I had a hard time sleeping, wondering what was wrong. I dozed off for a bit, then suddenly, I felt that exciting sensation come back, and as I jumped out of bed, confused and screaming. Tears coming down my face, and I felt like this was never going to end. I eventually had my wife take me to the emergency room, where I was diagnosed with having panic attacks.

Over the next few years, the doctors put me on medication. I had to see a therapist to help with my issues. Eventually, I overcame the attacks and have not had a significant episode in over ten years. Along with the Panic attacks I dealt with, I was also diagnosed with depression. I always felt I dealt with it, but I did not accept it until the doctors confirmed it. There would be days that I would not be motivated to do anything in life, but there was always a side telling me to get up and push myself, and it was never easy. I would lie in bed all day and stare at the walls thinking to myself, why did I have to deal with all this stuff, yes there was pain and helplessness, and feeling like no one in the world would ever understand what I felt. There were many times I would drink alone to deal with the pain just so I could carry on with my day, and I would hide it well.

I would be lying to you if I never said I wanted to end my life at times. The thought of suicide had crossed my mind, but I knew that I had way too much to live for, like my kids and my wife. I would look at myself in the mirror at times and tell myself I was disgusting, ugly, and no one cared about me. I could not stand to look at myself in the mirror, even in pictures, because behind the smiles in the photos were lies as no one knew what I was feeling on the inside. I guess because of what I was exposed to as a kid and a young adult, and what people also told me, I embraced it and believed it. Words can hurt, and the words you choose can either change someone's life or destroy someone's life, as it affected mine both ways.

UNDERSTANDING

I would always question why people are still walking away from me or not wanting to be friends. Is it me? Did I do something wrong? I just do not know. I once was told that I intimidate people. I have also been told that I am too nice, and this one is the best, I overpower people with my positive energies. It is something that has baffled me as a kid and as an adult. I was never the popular kid, never the athletic kid, or the most attractive or smartest kid. Sometimes I feel like I am alienated from the world and can only deal with selective people that understand me. I admit I could be difficult at times, but for the most part, I am an extremely easy going and loving person, and those that truly know me can back me on that. To this day, I would have to admit I have never been good at making friends or keeping friends.

People tend to come into my life for extended amounts or short amounts of time then walk away. I wish I could have people in my life that I was close to, hang out with and even call someone on the phone to say "hey," but that has never been a reality for me. It is not easy going through life, saying that I do not have a best friend or someone that can be there when you need to talk. Counseling was something that I had done from the age of 8 up to an adult off and on, but these people do not care too much for your issues. When your hour is up, and they take your money, then they will have to hear another sad story all over again. I am a big believer in "Season," "Reason," and "Lifetime." Here is how that works. A Season is someone that comes into your life for, say, 3 to 6 months or maybe a year. When these people come into your life, you must understand why you met them, what you need to learn from them or what you are supposed to leave them, then you never see them again. It is the same with "Reason," which could be a brief encounter, or a day or two, then never see them again. Then there is "Lifetime," These are the people that stay with you a lifetime, and you continue to learn, and you teach throughout your entire life.

When I entered the Military in 2000, I was shipped off to Army Basic Training in Fort Jackson, South Carolina. I met all kinds of people from all over the country. As soldiers, we became friends, and we became a family learning to accept each other. It took time to adjust to each other in 9 weeks because we were all from different cultures, races, denominations, and genders. I will never forget the day we graduated. We all stood around crying, not sure what we were supposed to do now that we had graduated. I only kept in touch with a few people, but what I learned from that experience was what it is like to have a family bond that could never be broken. Regardless if we did not like each other or not. I learned a lot about myself and other people and life. This was where my life started a slow turn to see the big picture. This was where I was beginning to "REACH." This was my "Season" lesson in life, I am sure I experienced many more, but this one stuck out the most and held close to my heart.

THE INTERNSHIP

While in college, I had to do an internship for the Radio Broadcasting program I was enrolled in. I ended up taking an internship with a station in Seattle at MIX 92.5 for the Mitch & Lisa Morning Show. I was so nervous and did not know what to expect, and I felt so ecstatic that I got the gig. Even after I left the program, my name would still float around the college's hallways like I was a legend or something.

I remember my first day walking into the radio station and thinking to myself, I made it. This is my opportunity to show the world that this kid overcame the odds. I felt like a kid in a candy store. The studio board lit up like a Christmas tree, and to be working on a morning show was incredible. I truly worked hard day and night, learning everything I could, and I would even come back later that night to teach myself things in the studio. I had a great time working on the show. I got to help with funny bits on the show, produce segments, and meet many celebrities that would stop by.

My first encounter with a celebrity was with Avril Lavigne. Now, remember this world was all new to me, and I was a bit culture shocked. I recall everyone was saying Avril Lavigne was going to be in for an interview this afternoon. She was a prominent POP artist at the time, and I was overly excited about my first celebrity sighting. I remember when she finally showed up, she was surrounded in a circle by band members and her management team. They stood in a corner while she was waiting for her interview in the hallway. I could not get a good glimpse because she had a hood on and was being incredibly quiet. As curious as I was, I tried my best to get a look. Eventually, I walked over, tilled my head to get a good look, and said hi to Avril. We locked eyes for a sec then a very odd silence as she and her band stared oddly at me. Thank goodness, the studio door opened at the time and said, "They are ready for you, Avril." The bell saved me, and I now have an everlasting impression of my first awkward celebrity moment to cherish.

As I was wrapping up my 3-month internship with the show and getting ready to graduate in a month from the radio broadcasting program, I learned a lot about the business and myself. I kept thinking to myself that I am here, I can make great things happen. I would sit alone and cry tears of joy because I now have the power and am gaining respect from my friends and family and the business for once in my life. I can proudly say that I'm still working in this business after 15 plus years and looking forward to another 15 years.

SLOW JAMS

As a kid, I always used to fall asleep with the radio on, and one of my favorite programs to listen to was Slow Jams. The music was the best, the people would call in to make dedications to their special someone, and I found a sense of comfort in it. There was a radio station in the mid-'80s called KSOL that had a Slow Jams show with host Marcus Gutierrez in the bay area. This guy was smooth on the microphone and had a voice that would command your attention on the airwaves. Every chance I got, I listened at night to hear my favorite songs that would take me away to another place and a distraction from my real world.

In 2006, I was offered a job at a new radio station in Seattle that just launched called MOViN 92.5. Its format was a mix of Top 40 hits mixed in with some '80s and 90's records with an urban feel. People loved it, and I loved it because it was right up my alley. I remember the station wanted to do something special for Valentine's Day, a night of slow jams and dedications, and I thought that would be great. It was during my shift, so they were going to have me do it. I was ecstatic and was pumped to do something on the radio that I grew up listening to and understood the groundwork for a show like this. At the time, the Program Director was a bit nervous about airing the program and said he would host it. I told him no, I wanted this shot to make something that I genuinely loved and had a passion for, slow jam music, and people. He agreed and let me do the show on Valentine's Day, and it was a success.

A few weeks later, I got a phone call from the General Manager and the Program Director on a 3-way call asking if I could do a weekly Slow Jams show during my shift. I did not hesitate and said yes. I thanked them for the opportunity and was extremely excited to do something that I grew up listening to and studied after all these years, and it paid off. The show took off like wildfire, there was no other kind of show like this in the Seattle market, and it launched my career into stardom. I was recognized as the Slow Jams guy everywhere I went. I got to host many concerts that came to the Seattle area, Bryan McKnight, Boyz II Men, Musiq Soul Child, and tons more. I felt like I was someone important for once in my life, a voice for people that did not have one when it came to love. I received emails and letters from people all over, including mail from Correctional Facilities. I do not think anyone realized the power of this show and what it did for people. It brought people together. It helped people, restored love in people, and thought I played a big part in that, and it was incredible.

The show stayed strong for about a year or two before the management decided to pull the plug. The station was moving in a different format direction and just was not a good fit anymore. Sad to say, shortly after the show was canceled, I was let go as well on the day before Thanksgiving. Let us say that is a Thanksgiving I will never forget. My heart hurt, and I felt like I did not try hard enough to keep the show alive. Many people were disappointed, and I received tons of emails and social media messages expressing their concerns. I felt a sense of disappointment that I let the people down. I went into hiding, I was depressed, and I felt my life went from everything back to nothing.

Me & Ludacris

Me & Naught By Nature

Me Serving My Country

My Dad The Marine

Baby Kaz

Me & My Mom

Me During The College Years

Me, My Wife & Daughters

Me & My Friend Robert

One of My Radio Head Shots

Me & G-Eazy

Me In The 8th Grade

Me DJing At The Club

Me & My Good Friend Shayn

Graduating The Academy

Me & Monti With Boyz II Men

WHO INSPIRES YOU?

How many people in your life can you say are mentors or people that encourage you in life? To some, there may be a lot. For others, few to none. I never really had anyone that cheered me on in life as a kid, and my encouragement came from what I saw on TV, in movies, the streets, and in real life. I looked up to all the wrong people in my life. I had friends and family members who thought to be successful was to do drugs, drink, rob, steal, and hurt others. As a kid growing up, I could not change what I saw in my own environment, but what I could change is how I saw my environment. As an adult now, I still never forget where I came from, my hardships, and lows in life. Those are all life lessons we take to make ourselves better and not only ourselves but for others around us in our lives or situation.

I want to tell you about a good friend of mine that I met when I was 19 years out, and His name is Shyan Selah. I do not think I ever met a person with so much drive to succeed and a passion for his craft and people. I met Shyan by accident one night at a music studio while he was in college. We were just two kids that wanted to make music. Shyan and I hit it off instantly when we met. We became good friends, and we learned the business together. Shyan showed me GOD, life, opportunities, and myself. Twenty-plus years later, Shyan and I are going strong and thriving in our own right. He now is the CEO of his successful entertainment firm, a musician, actor, community activist, and just an all-around good spirit and human being.

I would have to say that I owe a good portion of my success in life, career, and spirituality to my friend Shyan. He saw something in me that no one else did. He saw I had a talent that most did not recognize. He saw I would be someone in life. So, I go back to the question, "Who inspires you"? Thank you, Shyan, for your love and support, and know that I am genuinely grateful for what you have done and what you will continue to do in your life and for others. I Love you brother.

LOVE

The story I am about to tell you would change my life forever in a significant way and plays a big part in my success in life. When I tell people this story, they always are in awe, and they always say that it sounds like something from a movie. Was this a coincidence, or was it fate? I will let you be the judge.

What is LOVE? I never knew what it was or what it meant until I met a beautiful and lovely young lady named Tanya. I met Tanya through a friend of mine, J.C., whose family was friends with her family. Tanya was living in San Francisco on the Presidio, a military installation where her stepdad, who was in the Navy, was stationed at. She came from a big family and had two other brothers and three sisters. When I met her family, my instant thought was the "Leave It to Beaver" family, and her Mom even brought out cookies and snacks for us. That is how I saw it, but that was not the case, I found out later.

Back in the day, when I was growing up, we did not have cell phones. They were around but not like how they are today, so we had things called pagers. In my small group of friends, we all had our own number codes, so we knew who was calling when we paged each other. My code happened to be "187". One evening I was at my friend J.C.'s house, and he got a page from a weird number. He said to me, "Someone is using your pager code." He called the phone number, and it was his younger brother Drew at Tanya's house in San Francisco and needed a ride home. We wondered why his brother used my pager code, and then we realized it was the last three digits of Tanya's house number. As I was getting ready to walk out the door of J.C.'s house to head home, he asked if I wanted to go and pick up his brother with him. I said no, I think I am going to head home for the night. J.C. Then said, "there are girls there." I immediately changed my mind, and next thing you know, we were on our way into the city.

Have you ever heard people say you will feel that out of body experience when you meet the right person? Well, that day it happened to me, I kid you not, as we pulled up to Tanya's house, everyone was outside, and that is when I saw her for the first time. I asked J.C. who that was, and he said that's Tanya, she was the most beautiful girl I had ever seen in my entire life. Still to this day, I remember what she was wearing, a blue striped shirt with white pants and had sexy curly brown hair and the most beautiful blue eyes. I thought that I am way out of this girls' league and do not stand a chance. I was a short and skinny nappy-headed kid that was not at all attractive. We both came from two different worlds. My odds of even getting her to talk to me was about as good as me winning the lottery. I think we hung out for about an hour, then headed back to J.C.'s house. All I could think about was Tanya, and I told J.C. we got to hook up again.

About a week later, we all got together and hung out. I got to know more about her and thought she was terrific. Of course, I was curious about what she thought about me. I felt she was not even interested in me as she said she had a boyfriend. As weeks passed, we ended up hanging out and going places and doing things. We had a great time, but then Tanya hit me with some news that made my heart sink into my stomach. She said that she would be moving to Washington State in about two weeks. For once in my life, when I felt that something was going so right, it just went so wrong, but I was used to things like that happening to me, so it was not anything new. I think I saw her one last time before she left, but we never had an official goodbye as the next time I went to visit her at her home, it was empty. She had already moved. Remember, back then, we did not have Facebook, cell phones, or emails, so there was no way of contacting her. She was gone, I was sad and knew that I would never see this girl again.

One night I was cleaning out some stuff in my room and came across Tanya's phone number, not sure what it was, but something told me to call it. I picked up the phone and dialed, and all I heard was, "We're sorry the number you have dialed is no longer in service." As I was getting ready to hang up the phone receiver, I heard, "The new number is......," I was so excited and nervous at the same time. At the time, I was living with my sister Julie. She was married to a Marine that was getting ready to be stationed in Southern California. She asked if I wanted to move with her. I did not want to move to the L.A. area as I was trying to leave Oakland's streets behind. I wanted a new start in life. I wanted to get away from everything and start fresh.

Years earlier, my Mom had moved to Seattle and realized I had an option, Seattle or L.A., I chose Seattle for some crazy reason, but it proved to be my calling card.

On December 1st, 1993, it was a cold and dark raining night when I stepped off the plane in Seattle, Washington. The first thing I did was call Tanya, I kept that number in my wallet waiting to call her but did not have a reason to, but now I did. When I called her, she was surprised that I told her I moved to Washington State. I asked where she was living, she said in a city called Bremerton about an hour west of Seattle. I came to find out that she had an aunt who lived about 10 minutes from me, coincidence, or fate? I guess you can say the rest is history.

I ended up marrying this wonderful woman that taught me about love, family, and life and starting our own family with our two wonderful daughters Kaylie and Kristin. I thank GOD every day for bringing her into my life. Yes, we have had our ups and downs, our ins and out, but we stuck it out through it all, and I do not think there is anyone else I would rather go through life with than this amazing woman. Tanya accepts me for who I am, what I have accomplished, and my faults in life. She has always been by my side no matter what, and I am blessed to have such a wonderful woman that is a great Mother to my children, independent, strong, and loving.

EASY TARGET

I was never the most athletic, the most popular, or even good looking in school. It just seemed like life gave me the short end of the stick. Most of my friends had everything I wanted but could never get things like money, nice clothes, nice cars and they all had lots of friends. I felt like there was always a rain cloud following me everywhere I went and a sign around my neck that said, I am not cool. Every bad thing you could think of would find me.

I remember this one time I was walking to meet a female friend of mine to catch a movie. As I rounded this corner, Three Asian guys out of nowhere started beating on me. All I saw was a fist to my face, and next thing you know, I was getting a good ass whooping. I was not so upset that I was taking a beating by these three Asian guys, but was more upset that the cars on the main street were swerving around us, honking their horns telling us to get out of traffic.

The ladies were never my expertise, either. I never had female friends or even good relationships with them. After a while, I just realized it was me. I maybe had one or two relationships before settling down with my wife. If I did encounter women, they would see how easy of a target I was to do what they wanted or use me for any and everything I had, which at the time was not much. I put myself out there to be that target and did not even know it, I prayed to be an average person and live everyday life and do normal things like most, but in my reality, it just was not in the plan, at least not yet. Later in life, I found the problem. I was trying too hard to be someone I was not. I tried to fit in with others that I did not understand, let alone understand myself.

As an adult now, I know that this was all part of GOD'S plan, I knew that I would always question why this was happening, but if those things did not happen, I would not be the person I am today. I have learned to be who I am and who I am supposed to be. It is not about getting what you want but getting what you need in life. I have lived on both sides of the table, from being broke and having nothing to being well off and having it all. Life can be challenging, intimidating, and stressful, but the secret is not to become that easy target, do not focus on the wrong things in life. Focus on the right things you need in your life. Do not be something you are not, be you, do you, and you will see everything will fall in place, and for me eventually, it did.

HE'S DEAD

I think in life, there are things that you should never have to be exposed to as a kid and seeing someone gunned down is not one of them. I was living with my sister at the time in a city called Suisun, a small-town north of Oakland, about an hour away. I was home alone for the weekend as my sister and her husband went to L.A. to see some family. I lived in an apartment complex with them directly across from a mini mart. It was so close I could hear the "ding noise" when people would enter the store.

One night I walked over to the mini mart for some dinner, not knowing that in the next 2 minutes, someone was about to lose their life. As I walked out of the mini-mart, I noticed a guy and two girls talking loudly at the gas pump. I was not paying attention to the conversation as I was trying to mind my own business and was hungry. I made it back to the apartment, and as I was walking up the stairs, I still noticed that the guy and two girls were still talking loudly. At that moment, a car going unusually fast pulled up right next to them and shot the guy. I dropped the food that I had in my hand and ran into the apartment, slammed the door, and locked it. All I heard was screaming and the screech of tires pulling off. I ran into my room and tried to sneak a look out my blinds, shaking, not realizing what just happened. I saw the man hunched over the hood of the car and the two girls screaming, "NO, NO, NO He's dead."

The rest of the night, I sat in the dark in my room, just thinking. I was literally about 30 seconds away from possibly getting caught in the crossfire and might have been a victim myself. It was indeed an eye-opener, and I did not know how to react. What I did know was I was sick and tired of seeing things like this happening around me. I just wanted to get away from it all and never hear or see this type of stuff again. Moments later, the street lit up with police lights and noisy sirens that echoed the neighborhood. I am not sure what happened to those people, but my heart and prayers went out to them and their families.

A week later, I was driving in a nearby neighborhood and noticed police tape around a home in an area I passed by. I did not think anything of it until I turned on the local news and recognized the house on TV. Someone in retaliation gunned down the person who had gunned down the guy with the two girls at the mini mart.

I AM STAR

When I got my first full-time gig, I thought I was big-time. I got hired to be the first night host on a brand-new station in Seattle, WA called MOViN 92.5 in October of 2006. It was a short-lived ride, but I experienced a superstar lifestyle. I was making good money, I was making all kinds of friends, and I was reconnecting with people that I have not seen in years. I was getting all this attention and finally felt like someone for the first time in my life. I would party like crazy, spending money left and right, fancy dinners, shopping sprees with no care in the world. The attention I was getting was ridiculous. People wanted me to come to their clubs, and I was getting just about anything for free, anything you could think of, I was getting it.

I was so caught up that I did not look at the things that mattered in my life, like my family and my real friends, as I hurt them and neglected them, my ego was at an all-time high, and I suffered for it in the end. Having your own radio show five days a week and having one of the most extensive night ratings with a specialty show was big business, especially to the radio station. I was being called the "Slow Jam King of Seattle," it was a unique show, and the ladies loved it, and yes, they loved KAZ as well.

My life was great, I bought a condo, cars, and I recall when I did not have a place to live and had to walk everywhere, this was too real for me. Remember, I never experienced what it was like to have things, and I was a young buck new to the business.

The day I was told that "SLOW JAMS" was coming to an end and I was getting let go from the station, that is when the ride I was on came to a sudden stop and said it is time to get off. I went from everything to nothing, and I was right back where I started. In my mind, I was back in that old dingy basement in Oakland, just stripped from everything in life. It was like my world stopped, my phone did not ring anymore, people did not want me around, my bank account was in the minus, what happened? In a way, I am glad this happened because I got to see my real friends and family and my fake friends and family.

For the next six months or so, I lived on unemployment and doing odd jobs to get by and provide for my family. It was a low time in my life. I turned to alcohol and hiding in my room all day as I felt embarrassed and ashamed of how my life was going. The lesson I learned did not last forever, and I had to reevaluate my life and priorities. I had to put my ego in check and know that at any moment, knowing everything you have in life can be stripped from you without warning. Once again, this was all in GODS plan. I was being tested to see how I would handle it, as you can see, not very well. I had to sell my home, give up things that were not necessities in my life, and learn to become humble and understand myself again.

To this day, I will never forget where I am from and remember the struggles and heartache to get to this point in life. I promised myself never to put myself or my friends and family in that position again, as I think it hurt me more than anyone else in the world. I have forgiven myself and look at it as a learning experience. We are all stars in our own right, but the question is, how will you shine when you finally get the opportunity to show the world?

OFF THE CHAIN

Today, I love how people are taking more of an initiative to help kids and be more vocal about abuse, drugs, alcohol, and bullying. As a kid, I was bullied quite a bit and never had anyone to turn to. When I hear or see stories of kids being bullied, it hurts my heart as I was one of those kids who knew how they felt. I was picked on, and I had to carry people's books home, give them my lunch money, and anything else you could think of. I was scared to tell anyone fearing that it would worsen and come back on me even harder from the people who would bully me.

When I was in the 4th grade, I had some friends named Pete, Richie and Timmy, well I thought they were my friends, until one day they had a change of heart. For some reason, they ganged up on me at school and started pushing me around, threatening me, and calling me names. For most of the day, it went on, and I was terrified to tell anyone. It got to the point where I broke down and cried. I tried to give them my lunch money and garbage pail kid stickers to stop picking on me, which did not work. I could not take it anymore, and I hopped on my bike and rode home as fast as I could, crying the whole way home. As I was pulling up to my house, my Mom's boyfriend Joe was outside and said, "What are you doing? Why are you not at school"? With tears rolling down my eyes, I could barely talk, I said kids at school were bullying me. Joe looked at me, then looked at my bike and said, "You see that chain you lock your bike up with? Start swinging it like a crazy maniac if they pick on you again, now go back to school and stop crying".

As I rode my bike back to school, I was so scared to see Pete, Richie, and Timmy, knowing that they were going to laugh and pick on me again. Sure enough, as I got back to school, I saw them near the bike rack during recess, and they spotted me. They yelled at me and started to run towards me, as my heart started beating faster and faster, all I thought about was what Joe said about my bike chain. As the guys got closer and closer, I closed my eyes and started swinging that chain like a crazy cowboy with a lasso. They backed up for a second, and I was so mad, crying, and saying, "come on" at that moment, a teacher came over to see what was happening, and I said these guys were bullying me. That is pretty much how it ended.

The guys started to be a little nicer to me after getting in trouble and even got a phone call from their parents. I never knew what happened to those guys, but I hope they stopped picking on people or maybe got a taste of their own medicine. I continued to get bullied throughout elementary, middle school, and high school. I never really told anyone as I felt that they would not listen or care. Today I have no tolerance for people that get picked on or bullied as I was one of those kids, and I knew the feeling. If friends and family are bullying you, know you are not alone. Tell someone it is ok, do not become a victim, find the solution, and resolve it before it is too late.

WHAT IS REACH?

I regularly get asked what is "REACH"? It is a movement that I started to inspire people to show how easy it is to reach your goals and dreams. It is a simple word used in the human vocabulary a million times a day, yet we never notice what the word means. Have you ever been in the kitchen and tried to grab something off the top shelf that was just an arm's reach away but needed a little more height, so you grab a chair or climb on the counters? The same thing applies to achieving your goals and dreams. Everything in your life you want is at arm's reach, and all you need is that extra boost to get there.

I once saw a picture in a magazine of a cartoon character with a shovel digging a tunnel into a massive mountain of dirt. One side had the guy digging and on the other side was a huge diamond. You can tell he was digging for an exceedingly long time from the picture, but what it said was so accurate. It said never stop moving forward because you never know how close you are to the reward, not exact words but along those lines. I thought about that for a second and said to myself, we never know how close we are to our goals and dreams, but if you never start digging into that mountain, you will never know.

So, I encourage you to keep digging through your mountain. Along the way, you will hit many rocks, barriers, detours, darkness, but know there is a light on the other side with the reward of your goals and dreams. That feeling of accomplishment will be the most incredible feeling you will ever experience when you break through that mountain. The next time you grab something and are a little short, all you need is that extra boost and positive thoughts of encouragement. That is what "REACH" is all about.

THE TOY DRIVE

In December 2014, I joined up with Toys for Tots to help collect toys for children in need for the holiday season. It was probably one of the most rewarding things that I have done in my life. What made it special was it was something that I did all by myself. I had a DJ gig on the 13th of the month and thought I would tie in a Toy Drive event also, so I created the first-ever "REACH" Toy Drive. It took a lot to put it together, from promoting it to finding sponsors, giveaways, and so forth and so forth. I was determined to make this a success. I was up day and night on my laptop, making calls, getting the word out, and trying to get people involved. It was easier said than done as I was turned down left and right from friends, family, and business. Once again, I was determined to make this happen. I was not doing this as a publicity stunt. I was not doing this to get recognized or any of that. I was doing this to help kids that were not going to have any presents under the tree this year for Christmas. Then why were you doing this? I was asked many times. I will tell you why, because I was one of those kids that did not have a Christmas one year and it was the worst Christmas ever that I will never forget.

We must go back to December of 1992. I was living in Oakland with my brother Bill, and if you recall, we were broke, no food at times, no electricity, and my brother was at an all-time low doing drugs. That might have been the first year I woke up Christmas morning to no tree, no presents, and no family. It was just another day, it seemed, but as I woke up and looked out the window, I saw the smiles of other people with their family's laughing and enjoying Christmas day. My brother walked into the room and said, "Merry Christmas," handed me a chocolate bar and an unwrapped CD form "Body Count," then left to go who knows where. I cannot recall what I did for the rest of the day, but I know I spent it alone.

So why did I do the Toy Drive? Because I was one of those kids. I know it was not much, but I collected 200 toys and about $130.00 in cash. It was a great night, but I felt it could have been better. I guess not too bad for putting it together in 2 weeks. The bottom line is that I took that step to help better other people's lives that Holiday season and cannot wait to do it again.

THE "E" WORD

The "E" word, I feared it all my life and was never good at it, "Education." Today, when I talk with kids or even my kids, education is more important than you even know. Growing up, I never had a good foundation for support of my education. I was acting up and not caring about school in the 5th grade, imagine going through life with a 5th-grade education. I was never thinking about the future throughout my whole ordeal in school, and I was always thinking about the "Now." I did not have a support system in school or at home. I found out in the 9th grade that I had ADHD, a learning disability, by then, it was too late to get the proper help I needed.

I ended up dropping out of school in my first week in the 11th grade. I was way too far behind and felt there was no way I would make it plus, at age 16, living on my own, there was no hope. Throughout life, it was hard to find a decent job. I worked in fast food, janitorial, warehouse, it just seemed like no growth or movement, and I was stuck. It was two life-changing events that got me back on track to better myself and get that education I truly deserved.

I want to tell you about one of the most wonderful ladies I met and took me in when I had nowhere to go. Her name was Eleanor, my wife Tanya's Mother, and she had the kindest and most loving spirit and soul. She allowed me to live with her family and treated me like a son. I was no different than any of her other kids. I loved talking with her about life, the future, and of course, helping me find my purpose. She stressed the importance of finishing my education. She helped push me to get my G.E.D., which I did accomplish in 1997, which was the same year Eleanor told her family that she had breast cancer. A year later, she passed away in late January of 1998, it was devastating to her family, and my heart still goes out to them.

Sometimes people come into your life to leave you with something. Eleanor left me with more than I could even fathom. I learned about family, love, and believing. I can genuinely say she played a massive role in that. Thanks to her, I completed my G.E.D. I went on to college, graduated with an A.A. in Radio Broadcasting, and continue to educate myself each day of my life. Please believe me when I say finish your education. Everything can be taken away from you in this world, but one thing that no one can ever take from you is your knowledge and education. Eleanor, thank you for believing in me and loving me like one of your own. I love you Mom and miss you each day.

CLOSING:

If my life and career ended today, I would have to say that was one hell of a ride. I tell myself each morning when I wake up that I am proud of myself, I am proud that I never gave up. As many times as I wanted to give up, there was always something telling me do not stop reaching. Never in a million years what I have thought about what I accomplished in life would have happened. I was just a kid that came from nothing and made something. I was bullied, beat, unloved, and lost in life. These experiences molded me into the person I am today, and as crazy as it sounds, I thank GOD for those experiences.

As we all know, everything in life comes to an end, good or bad. After the bad comes the good, After the rain comes the sunshine. Just because you may be stuck in a particular situation in life right now does not mean it will always be like that. If there is something you genuinely want to do in life, go for it. We, ourselves, are the only people stopping us from what we want in life. Making that first step to change in life can be terrifying. I know, you think about what people will say, you think about failing, and you think about not making it. Well, here is an eye-opener for you, failing in life are only steps to success, and do not worry what other people think about what you're doing, be yourself, do you, go for the gold. I know you probably heard it a million times from people about reaching for your goals and dreams, and you ask yourself, what do these people know about my dreams and goals? I was one of those people that questioned it all the time.

If there is one thing that I want people to take from this book is that you can do it regardless of where you are from, your background, or what you have been told all your life, I am living proof of that. I removed myself from certain situations in life, made the best of what I thought was terrible, and made an excellent opportunity. Do not be afraid to try, do not be scared to fail, remember those are only steps to success. Be around the right people that believe in you and encourage you, it only takes one person to make those dreams and goals come to life, and it starts with you. Let us start today. All you must do is "REACH" I promise you that it is all you must do in life to make it, and remember, I am cheering you on every step of the way to life's finish line. Now go "REACH" I believe in you.

A unique show playing classic hits of the late 80's and early 90's R&B, Hip-Hop from the "NEW JACK SWING" era. Featuring artists such as Keith Sweat, Guy, New Edition, Janet Jackson, Heavy D, SWV and much more. The program will take listeners on a journey back to reminisce about special memories or moments through the magic of music, interviews, TV and movie clips from the era.

Make sure to check out **NEW JACK RADIO WEEKLY**
A nationally syndicated radio show hosted by djKAZ
as he takes you back to the 80's & 90's with R&B and
Hip Hop hits of the NEW JACK SWING era.
Check to see if your local radio station is airing
NEW JACK RADIO WEEKLY w/djKAZ or go to
www.newjackradiolive.com for more information.

Made in the USA
Columbia, SC
10 July 2024

38451410R00039